LEAP
off the
LADDER

From Corporate Life to Pursuing
Your Own Path

By Morgan Chavis

Contents

DEDICATIONS..5
INTRODUCTION 7

CHAPTER 1
ORDERED STEPS.. 19

CHAPTER 2
SECOND GUESSING.. 25

CHAPTER 3
DIVING IN 31

CHAPTER 4
CHALLENGES 47

CHAPTER 5
LITTLE BLACK BOOK... 59

CHAPTER 6
THE ROLODEX 63

CHAPTER 7
THE BEST PART... 69

DEDICATIONS

Philippians 2:13

To My Husband,

Thank you for teaching me what support means. Words simply cannot express the gratitude I have for you. From endless nights talking about plans for my business, to listening to my ideas for the book and working on the cover together you have pushed me each step of the way. You have wiped my tears on days where it all felt too difficult and encouraged me to persevere. I cannot imagine taking this leap without you hand in hand. I hope you are proud and understand that this is an accomplishment we have achieved together.

To the Lusso Salon Team,

It is full of emotions that I dedicate this to you all. None of this would be possible without each of you. You have rallied with me through numerous life changes and countless twists and turns with this business. With every twist you each have encouraged me to keep going! Each of you pushed me to leap off the ladder even when I was too scared to even think of going for it. You have all brought me your bright ideas that have made Lusso Salon what it is today and celebrated my every milestone with joy. The success of this business has never stopped at me; it is about each one of you. God has placed you each in my life for a purpose. You've taught me dreams really can come true! To every client who has supported us all, we thank you. Many of you have sat in my chair or in the chairs around me and contributed to my many ideas. Your well wishes and encouragement push me to keep achieving more. This accomplishment is dedicated to you, the supporters of my dreams!

To My Dad,

Your love, encouragement and demand for greatness have elevated me to heights I didn't have to wonder whether I could achieve because you already instilled in me that I could. You taught me there is no limit to what I can do and would accept nothing less than greatness. Thank you for molding me into who I am today. In my wildest dreams I hope to be as great of an entrepreneur as you are. All that I do is to make you proud.

To My Friends and Family,

My tribe is deep! My tribe is supportive! You have been patrons before the business was even a business. You all are my biggest cheerleaders and I thank you for supporting me from day one.

"Cowgirl Up!" - Sylvia W. Wilson

INTRODUCTION

Nothing happens if you don't get started. I am forever buying these cute little notebooks with an "M" on them for Morgan, planners, and goal pads… so much so that I want my own retail product line of them. One day, I used one of those cute notepads to write down my judgment-free list of goals. Of course, my educational background in business management tells me all these dreams should be written as "SMART" goals, But this time, I said, FORGET IT. I just wrote:

1. Podcast
2. Book
3. Speaking engagements
4. Business Consultant
5. Franchise suites
6. Consistent eCommerce revenue of $10k/mo (This was almost a SMART goal. I can't help it.)
7. Reality TV Show cast member
8. Ted Talk presenter
9. Online classes

10. 800+ credit score
11. Usable business credit
12. Purchase car under my business name only
13. Have a personal assistant
14. Blue check on IG
15. Host charity gala
16. Business planning stationery product line
17. Hampton University Top 40 Under 40 Alumna

I tried to leave money out of it. I didn't want to write down financial goals like, "get liquid savings to $xxxx or have $xxx... net worth". I just wanted to write down what I would like to occupy my work week or what I'd be happy to consume in my everyday life. I didn't put family goals, marriage goals, or goals as a mother. I didn't set a retirement age or an earnings goal. I didn't worry about "the how" for any of them either... yet. For now, I just wrote down my dreams no matter how "unSMART" they were. I didn't share the list with anyone but my husband. I didn't want the judgment of how the list made me look or the laughter of anyone wondering why I would like to be a reality T.V. cast member. I just wanted to be me and run my race without judgment. Then one day, while watching one of my favorite reality shows, I started thinking about the hows.

"How did these women get here." I googled "How to get a blue check on Instagram." I instantly got overwhelmed. I mean, that's exactly why studies show that we should make SMART goals: specific, measurable, attainable, realistic, and timely". These goals demonstrated none of that. They aren't specific, nor are there dates on which I want to reach benchmarks that would get me to any of these goals to measure against for success. The entire list was just my pipe dreams.

That's when it hit me; these aren't goals but dreams. It hit me like a truck. To this point, I have been plowing through my dreams, checking them off a list like they were goals, but they aren't. They are my aspirations hence my motivation. They are meant to be abstract and obscure. They are intended to be in the stars. They are meant to be unrealistic. They are designed to drive my actions. I got off my couch in my lounge, a checkmark of mine from a few years ago, and grabbed my husband's laptop (you'll know the reason for this later), and I started writing this book. I came to the realization that these dreams of mine will always seem unreachable if I don't just start! I have no freaking clue how to write a book, but here we go...

I got my start in Detroit, Michigan. It wasn't until I moved away from Detroit that I realized how much being born and raised there molded so much of me. My parents raised me in one beautiful tutor-styled home in one of Detroit's historic neighborhoods on the westside for most of my life. Though Detroit is my home, it isn't my parent's home, so I feel like my roots took me all across the country and influenced me early to adapt to different people and environments. My dad is from Gary, Indiana. His dad is from Mississippi but raised most of his adolescent life in Chicago and Gary. His career took him to many places, but he has called Los Angeles, California home for longer than my life. My mom was born and raised in Houston. She and my dad met there while he lived there for work. Like my grandfather, his career took him to many places too, but his moving truck stopped in Detroit shortly before I was born. I never experienced packing and moving as a child as my older sister did. This is the start of my yearning for stability in routine behaviors. I went from cradle to college in the same bedroom. I have always been ambitious, and I was born an entrepreneur. My sister is eight years older than I am. When she would have her friends over, I would make them unknowingly sign a contract to play with me. I would write on my construction paper with a crayon, "A Play Contract," and I would scribble illegible words to make them sign what they thought was a senseless, pretend contract from a first grader. I'd go in my room after they signed and cut their signature off the bottom, then glue it to a contract where I'd made them agree to play with me for x amount of hours for the day. Dare they not comply with my play contract? I would have a tantrum. I was born a saleswoman. At age 12, I took a babysitting class and got a CPR certification. My mom helped me create a website, business cards, and a brochure marketing my babysitting services to all their friends and our neighbors. I told them I was certified through Girl Scouts of America, CPR trained, and I even came with my suitcase full of puzzles, games, and crafts to do with their kids to set me apart; of course, that came at a premium price. As a kid, I never spent a day without a couple of dollars in my pocket. I have always wanted to be a cosmetologist and own a beauty brand. My parents supported me from day one. I was "Morgan's Mane Styles". I had a full beauty salon setup in my basement where I'd take all my parents' friends' children for services, my mom and my sister as paying clients. My grandfather affectionately shares pictures of me in a pull-up in our Detroit home's sunroom, standing on the coffee table, styling my late Grandma Peggy's hair with Leggos. This dream for me never changed. I will never forget my first day working in a salon at age 13. My mom helped me call all the salons near us she found suitable from the yellow pages, asking if they were hiring a shampoo girl. Most said no when they found out how old I was, but one did not, Megan Mitchell's Hair Studio in Ferndale, Michigan. Megan Mitchell, the owner, told me to come on in with my mom that weekend so she could hear me out. I was so thrilled. I spent the entire week preparing my portfolio with Polaroid pictures of my work and descriptions of my skill sets. On the big interview day, my mom drove me to the salon and introduced herself to Megan. From there, she let me speak for myself. I'd created a resume, brought my most recent report card, and showed her my pictures. With my mom's blessing, she offered me a job to work every Saturday morning as long as I was reliable, open to learning, and kept a positive attitude. My mom agreed she would get me to work, but the scary part for me was my dad's blessing. I participated in musical theater, dance, cheerleading, and pageants at the time. I needed to drop something to make my shampooing career work, but I was determined. When I came home, my mother forced me to speak with my dad about this. I gave him a full sales pitch with an analysis of the advantages of my newfound income and the transferable skills I'd gain. He agreed to my job as long as "those grades better not drop at that school I pay for." I immediately called my grandfather and told him the great news! My mom took pictures of me in front of the salon sign on Nine Mile Rd on my first day of work in the outfit I meticulously picked from Limited Too. I never looked back. Megan was a mentor to me. She showed me many things about haircare and using professional products, and she used my skills as a millennial to manage her front end and inventory. I created a tracking system for her product ordering and started collecting client emails for marketing. I never got too tired to wake up early on Saturday morning for my job. I loved being there. I loved learning from all the cosmetologists and experiencing servicing clients. I stayed at that job for my entire high school career. It confirmed that my dreams of being a salon owner were what I wanted to do with my life. I was just getting started.

In tenth grade, I asked my dad if I could attend

cosmetology school at night. My mom took me to the suburbs to Pivot Point Cosmetology School in Novi, Michigan. The program cost nearly $10,000 and would take me the remainder of my high school career to complete. From where I lived in Detroit, it was about a 40-minute drive and even further from my school. Classes were four days during the school week from 5 pm to 9 pm and every other Saturday. This is what I wanted to accomplish with my life; I knew it. I needed my dad to believe in me. His answer was a stern "no." I did not live in poverty at all, which is what many people think when they hear I lived in the heart of the city. My neighborhood was one of many gems in Detroit. It was a golf club community between Six Mile and Seven Mile of upper-middle-class families and was predominantly black. My grandmother would make a statement to describe my neighborhood, "You don't live in the hood, baby, but you can smell it from the front porch." Though the neighborhood was nice, the community was still that of inner-city Detroit, with some of the worst schools in the city. My dad was paying tuition of about $18,000 a year for me to attend an illustrious private school, University Liggett (School) in Grosse Pointe Woods, Michigan, an upper-class suburb. My school was a 35-minute commute east of my home. So asking to not only attend evening school but add additional tuition was insane to my dad. It would also mean that I could no longer participate in extracurricular activities. My dad was setting me up to be competitive enough to attend any college I wanted, and more importantly to him, he was setting me up to earn a scholarship to college, hopefully. For these reasons, he decided that I could not attend cosmetology school. I felt like my dreams were being crushed. In my teenage brain, my dad was not supportive of my dreams and didn't understand who I wanted to be. I thought he wanted me to be just like him and wanted no other path for my life. At that time, he was my villain. Tragedy struck my family after my junior year of high school when my mother unexpectedly died. She was my biggest fan, my forever client, my cheerleader, my motivator, and at the time, one of the only people I thought understood me. My older sister was married and living in Los Angeles near my grandfather. So this left me home in Detroit with just the villain. My earth was shattered. In my grief, I wondered why God took my mother from me when it felt like I was just getting started. You know, people say, "everything happens for a reason." I could not find a reason for the loss of her young life. I've come to find a reason now. God took my mother from me to bring my dad and me closer together. We were all we had in what was once a full home. I spent so much time giving him attitude and being sour about the choices he made for me. Now he and I had to support each other through a loss no one could see coming. My dad took me to every college I wanted to tour all on his own. He helped me complete every entrance application and essay. He took me to all of my grief counseling appointments, to church every Sunday, to choose a prom dress, and consoled my tears after my first heartbreak. As much as I felt he did not understand me, I learned I was wrong. He was preparing me to live the life of my dreams. He pushed me, sometimes too hard, to be successful and self-sufficient. He loved me unconditionally, and I could see it as we both had to endure life in our home together. He became my best friend. My grades suffered throughout my senior year of high school without my mom, my focus on various activities wavered, and I struggled with severe depression. My performance made me ineligible for any college scholarships to which I applied. Luckily, my dad encouraged me to apply for early decision entry to the colleges I wanted to attend, and I am so happy I did. In November of my senior year of high school, I received the first acceptance of many from my alma mater, Hampton University. I remember my dad and I celebrating after getting the letter in the mail. I was worried without the scholarships my dad preached about my whole life, this would no longer be an option for me, but my dad told me he would do whatever it took to send me to the college of my choice, and he did just that. By January, I committed and enrolled in pre-college to start a semester early. I was ready to leave Detroit and leave what felt like a haunted house I lived in without my mother. Hampton University was my hope during a dark time. I knew if I could finish, I would be off to Hampton only two weeks after the graduation ceremony. After four short weeks into the early summer semester, I told my dad during our daily morning phone call that I'd applied for a job at a nearby hair salon to work for a Hampton alumna. He fell silent on the phone. I knew what that meant. He was concerned about my grades, balancing my school work, and enjoying a full college experience while working. I knew he was also concerned about how I would handle grieving my mother's death in a new place alone after only a year, but things were different now. I was no longer in Detroit and was "grown," so I did it anyway. Every Saturday morning, I took the yellow cab from campus to work for Hairista Studio as an assistant, doing hair in-between times in my dorm. My dream never changed. It was the start of my junior year in college when I told my dad I found a cosmetology school that would be flexible with my packed schedule. At this point, I was an overachiever in many leadership roles in various student activities on campus. My dad met me with the same energy he did when I was in high school. "I am paying all this money for you to get a job after college. You're going to get distracted and lose your leadership position. I'm not paying for this". This time, the difference was that I wasn't asking for his permission or money. I was telling him this was what I was going to do, and I planned to style enough hair to pay for it. I was just getting started! I enrolled at Beyond Beauty Academy under Dr. Latonya Taliferro as one of the very first students of her freshly accredited beauty program. I already knew how to style hair, but Dr. T, who I affectionately call Ms. Tonya, taught me how to be a cosmetologist. She taught me the hair business. She showed me how to manage a clientele and how to retain them. She groomed me into a professional at my craft. She helped me to take hair from a hobby to a career. I proved my dad wrong. I completed cosmetology school and passed the state board exam two weeks before Hampton's graduation, making it a double ceremony. I was a highly decorated graduate with several honors and a robe stuffed with cords; however, this was the first in my life, and I was perplexed about what direction to go with my career after graduation.

CHAPTER 1

ORDERED STEPS

Our path is always easier when steps are ordered. From middle school, we know high school is next. It just is. After high school, I knew college was next. That was not my pivotal moment of steps not being ordered, though it is for some. College was a no brainer for me. I knew I wanted to attend a top HBCU and study business management. I had no doubts about that. I was fortunate to study abroad for a J-term during my senior year at Hampton. I called my dad, begging again for the funds to go. We agreed that he'd pay the money for the program's costs, and I'd be responsible for my spending. Family members and friends sent me money to help, and I was off to Greece! I took an international business class there and spent a few weeks exploring different European cities. Of course, with my dad being who he is, he insisted I not leave for Greece without post-graduate job interviews lined up. I complied with his request. A few days before my planned departure, I got a job offer from Target Corporation to be an entry-level distribution-center manager in Southern Virginia. Now let me tell you, I LOVE my HBCU, but I was by no means a fan of Virginia. I felt it was slow and boring in comparison to Detroit, and I knew leaving the ameba - a private college campus - would subject me to the country living Virginia had to offer. Whenever asked, I told everyone I was on the first plane smoking out of Virginia after college graduation. Luckily, I was given time to respond to my job offer; given that I was headed to Greece, the corporation graciously allowed me to accept the offer upon my return. Talk about the place to soul search! I truly felt conflicted. My steps were not ordered. This wasn't my dad's decision, it was mine. Ms. Tonya had a full-time position waiting for me at her salon as a licensed cosmetologist, and I had already grown the clientele to sustain booth rent. I was also conflicted about leaving Virginia and moving to a more fun city. I considered Washington D.C., which has always been a place I loved, Houston with my mom's family, and now my sister lived there, Los Angeles with my grandfather, Chicago near Gary with my dad's family, or even home to Detroit. The world was my oyster, literally, and that was the problem. I had too many options to make a decision. For once, upon asking my dad what I should do, he chose this time not to give his opinion. Convenient... I took a journal with me to Greece and wrote about all the cool experiences I had. I wrote my prayers in that journal and my dreams. During my J-Term, I spent a weekend in Italy, my mom's favorite country. There, I sensed her presence and thought I could hear her. It was in Italy that I decided it was not yet time for me to leave Virginia, and it was also not time for me to be a full-time cosmetologist. For the first time, I chose something other than hair. I called my dad, but the time difference was not in my favor, so I didn't get an answer. It's probably a good thing I didn't because I impulsively emailed the recruiter from Target, accepting the job offer from my bed in Greece. I knew this decision meant being a full-time cosmetologist, and this was not in the cards. At the time, it felt like a permanent decision. It felt like I was quitting on hair, quitting on my dreams. I should have been so excited to have a post-graduate job offer in the bag before even the final semester of my college career began, but I wasn't. Part of me felt like I was giving up on myself and what I wanted. I started at Target, eager to learn. I got an apartment in the city where my job was, and for the first time, without a roommate. Of course, my dad helped me move in and get settled. I was thrilled on my first day of work, but it didn't take long for me to miss the salon. In my true fashion, I called Ms. Tonya and asked for my booth. She asked me the golden question, "how are you going to work here and there." I told her I didn't know, but I would. I eventually did, and it was a struggle. I was exhausted, commuting far and losing clients. My poppin' college clientele had relocated to various cities after graduation. Many of them went to Washington, D.C. I spent many weeks using my money from my Target job to pay my booth rent at the salon because my services were barely breaking even. It's a privilege to say this was my first time experiencing failure, and I took it hard. I took this roadblock as a sign that hair was not for me. Ms. Tonya saw that I'd lost my spark completely. She calls me "Mini Me." One day she called me into her classroom and said, "Mini-me, what are you doing here? What is the problem?" I told her this was no longer my calling and I needed to dream a new one. I was doing well at Target, and I liked my job. Maybe my dad was right; I needed to focus on a corporate career path. She told me I was working hard and not smart. She said, "if your clientele has relocated, you need to relocate too." I couldn't believe it. I thought she would be disappointed in me for planning to leave her salon, but she wasn't. She wanted to see me win instead. I'd always had the support of my family through anything, but this was the first time I truly understood support from a mentor. I took her advice and found a salon in the heart of Washington D.C. on U Street to service my clientele. I worked at Target and drove 3 hours on the weekends to service clients' hair. When I arrived in town, I'd stay at my Aunt Delphia's house and party with my friends after work. I'd hit the road in time to get to Target for my first-week shift. Now I felt like I was living the dream! I was also making some pretty good money for a 22-year-old. All seemed well, but my steps still weren't ordered.

    I started getting tired. My clients were tired of only being able to have appointments crammed on one day of the week, and I was ready for a change. I was making good money, and I was spending it too. I was building a wardrobe of high-end designer fashions, constantly taking international trips with my friends, and making irresponsible decisions with my little coins that felt big at the time. School life felt more straightforward than this, so I applied for a few

MBA programs. It was to my surprise that my dad said if I wanted to go back to school, I had to pay for it and continue to work. I don't know why I thought otherwise. With that news, I never even opened my decision letters as they arrived in the mail.

I was lost and was super ready to leave Virginia. Work was getting more intense, but I was handling it well. I decided it was time to stop driving to D.C., so I left my now small clientele behind to focus on my corporate career. No one prepared me for the consequences of having an apartment, not on a college campus. I got a letter about a rent increase that I honestly could not afford with my lifestyle. It was time for me to put some big girl pants on and make decisions about my life. I decided graduate school was not it and did not want student loans. I decided hair wasn't it because I had mismanaged my clientele; therefore, I no longer had one. I decided that Corporate America was working out for me. I was assigned some projects at work that were promising. I made some close friends from work, so I had a social life that no longer put me on the highway or the plane. I also started dating Zach, now my husband, whom I met at work. I would never have thought it to be so, but I chose to purchase my first home in Virginia and stick with my job. I used all my savings and some to buy a townhouse in Southern Virginia.

Why did I think my steps were ordered now? They weren't. I just knew. I had a plan, and it wouldn't change anymore. Things were going great between

Zach and I, and we spent all our free time together. I was sometimes traveling, but I could also save money. My mortgage payment was much lower than my rent, so I was making better decisions with my income, but something still wasn't right. I didn't like my job and was just good at it. I was unfulfilled. This wasn't my dream, but I didn't realize yet that was the issue. I applied for some new jobs. I left Target and went to Amazon, which was like the ultimate sin to them at the time. I was searching for something that would work for me and make me happy. I was lost. Remember that list of dreams I had? Nowhere on it did it say, "work for someone else." That's not it for me. I spent five years hopping around the rungs of many different ladders at Amazon to realize, "this ain't it."

Zach and I got married in 2019 while I was at Amazon. We are the two crazies who also decided a few months later, as newlyweds, it was my time to follow my dreams and open a salon. Lusso Salon was born on September 1, 2019. At this time, I was still a Senior Manager at Amazon, now a mom and a wife, and I was not even doing hair, so there was no clientele. I networked, built a team, and grew a profitable business with the support of my husband. We shook the table completely when I resigned from a six-figure job to be a full-time entrepreneur after two years of managing both Lusso Salon and my Amazon career. Now everyone, especially my dad, thought I was nuts.

CHAPTER 2

SECOND GUESSING

Writing that resignation letter was challenging. It was different from leaving Target. I wasn't going to a competitor, I was going to be my own boss. I had some savings to supplement the considerable income drop in front of me and the support of my husband to make up for my gaps in household contributions if we needed to pull that lever. So why was this hard? Working for the world's largest company and performing well is the ultimate job security. Why would I leave a monthly check and stock bonuses for a career that was just completely shut down during the pandemic? Am I insane? I started to second-guess everything. Why did I even go to college? Did I waste my time? Did I waste my dad's money? Why did I even work for Amazon or Target? Am I a wasted hire? Am I a waste of talent? Second-guessing became my favorite hobby. I remembered telling my dad I was ready to leave Amazon. He told me every reason he could find to make me change my mind.

To him, my business was still a side hustle that only aided in financing shopping and travels with friends. He mentioned that I would no longer have support from an HR team or a host of direct reports like I did at Amazon, and all would be on me. What my dad didn't realize was that it was already confirmed. Lusso Salon was open and operating for two years. I managed the business dually employed, survived the pandemic, had a happy team with impeccable retention, and was still a Senior Manager. My husband and I had just purchased a new home, our "forever" home. My dad was worried that I wasn't prepared for the impact of my change in income. Indeed, I wasn't.

I assumed I understood everything. I gave myself one year to close my income gap. That was completely unrealistic. I learned the hard way that being an entrepreneur is not about planning to succeed; it's about planning to fail. That sounds morbid, but it is true. Who makes a plan not to be profitable? Who plans to struggle to pay their bills? We are always going to think of best case scenario. As an entrepreneur, you have to prepare for the worst. Plan for no customers, plan for no staff, plan for no online orders, plan for no leads, plan for no revenue. There aren't any rules. No one owes you a patron of your business. There will be weeks that completely suck where there isn't enough money flowing in. That's what you need to plan for.

I had already experienced many of these "what ifs," but I experienced them all with the life jacket of my Amazon income. In the weeks or months that the salon fell short, I pulled from my savings to recover, or I wouldn't pay myself for my clients and sales at the salon. If we needed something I didn't budget or plan for, I would buy it knowing I was getting another check from that six-figure income soon enough. I was completely unaware of how comfortable that life jacket made me. It wasn't until now that I asked myself, have I been swimming or just wading in the water? All these scary thoughts didn't keep me from jumping to the deep end without the life jacket because I am writing this as a business owner and CEO of Lusso Salon and its subsidiaries. Before I resigned, substantial consideration was given to whether or not to do so.

I resigned from Amazon on July 8, 2021, with a 30-day notice. The first bill I could not pay arrived in the mail in January of 2022. I had a complete meltdown. Never in my life was I unable to pay a bill. Not when I was in college doing hair in my free time, not when I was working for Target and spending money like a mad woman at every mall, and especially not while I was working for Amazon and in a partnership with a supportive man. I felt like I failed. I exhausted nearly 50% of the timeline I gave myself to rebound my income, and I was far from achieving that goal. Instead, I was at what felt like an ultimate low. It took some accurate personal reflection to dig myself out of this rut because, at the moment, I thought this was rock bottom. I thought I had made the dumbest decision and started looking for jobs. Still, each job description I found for roles that I'd easily qualify for, as I had the experience, sounded like something I had already done before and hated or didn't want to do. None of them had my passion tied to them.

I realized I had to find a stride. I was making it through the day-to-day, but I had no rhyme or reason for my actions. There were no routine or operating standards, only fighting fires as they came. Part of me was enjoying the change in pace for a moment. It was nice not to juggle two jobs for once or work a crazy amount of hours in one day. It took me some time to realize that I was enjoying the pleasure of a little moment of rest rather than feeling worn out all the time. Climbing the corporate ladder did not come without stress, nor did running a brick-and-mortar business. I also realized I needed to push myself with my business then. I'm a firm believer in therapy. Everyone should have a therapist. In one of my sessions, I talked about this guilt I was having for leaving the salon on an eight-hour day and not taking work home or not working on my expansion planning. My therapist helped me sort out what was happening in my head during this time. I was exhausted and honestly taking a break.

Please do yourself a favor, and don't feel guilty about it! Why should I supplement one unsustainable pace of juggling two jobs with the untenable idea of driving myself to the ground as an entrepreneur? I needed a moment to exhale and put my shoulders down during one of the most challenging transitions of my life to date. I needed the opportunity to feel like the walls weren't inching toward me, ready to crush me in the middle. I didn't have the mental space to expand or analyze waste then. I just needed to "be." I needed to be proud of myself for my courage to quit. I needed to be accustomed to the absence of a financial safety net. I needed to be comfortable manipulating my schedule, no one was required to approve. I needed to be ok with the unknown and give myself grace in the time it would take me to get there.

CHAPTER 3

DIVING IN

Anyone who tells you they have no regrets in their entrepreneurship journey is telling a bald-faced lie! I learned a lot with my start, and among the most frequent inquiries I get is, "what are your biggest lessons learned?". So why not air them in this book?

Managing Your Investment Capital

You'll need money to start your business, whether from a loan, a grant, savings, an investor, or a miracle lottery ticket. No matter where that money came from, your goal has to be to earn it back and then some (which would be profit). My dad always says, "a business that makes no money isn't a business; it's a hobby." I want to think he is right on that one. My startup money for my business was money I saved from my corporate work compensation. I remember like it was yesterday, when I walked into the Bank of America branch near my home to deposit a check I wrote to my LLC in the amount of all my startup money I'd saved. The teller looked at the statement and said, "Wow, you own a salon near here?". I explained to her that I would be opening my salon in a few months. She could read the body language, and I was so nervous handing her that check. She even commented on the amount of money and told me I should be proud of myself. I couldn't accept the compliment because I was scared shitless and knew all that money was already spent. My savings I worked so hard to earn were going to be gone in the next 30 days on furniture and equipment for the salon, security deposits on my space, marketing materials I planned to purchase, and all my utility startup fees. I didn't see that as an accomplishment at the time. I saw it like I was making myself broke! Who does that?! I learned that the mindset you keep is the result you will reap. I was NOT going broke; I was investing in myself and a business I knew I would make successful. Starting with the mindset of failure and the idea that taking risks is idiotic is self-sabotage. How do we expect to withstand the peaks and valleys of business if we don't believe the bet will be worth the reward? There isn't anything wrong with nervousness or even fear, but I learned that it is different from self-sabotage. Anxiety gives us the pressure we need to produce the diamond. Self-sabotage makes us doubt our decisions, operate in fear, avoid healthy risks and move with uncertainty.

Ok, so back to that check I deposited... lots of lessons learned with that, baby! I had a spreadsheet of projected costs and spent every dime of the bill. That was dumb. There will always be expenses we don't realize will be incurred until they slap us in the face.

Odds are the money you have saved, earned, borrowed, or won from the miracle lottery ticket to invest in your business is going to be a more considerable lump sum of money than you are used to managing on a day-to-day basis or one which you've ever had to manage at once in your life tangibly. I know it was for me. My instinct was to have a plan for every penny, but in hindsight, I don't think that was the best way to do things. When opening my salon, I had a plan but no team yet. I just knew from working in the industry what things were marketable to captivate and hire stylists, and I knew I could make Lusso Salon an excellent workplace.

All I needed was the opportunity to talk with them about my plans and give my pitch. I knew I could build a team, and I wasn't wrong. Once I paid the security deposit at my first salon location, which a previous salon owner subleased to me, I started furnishing it and making it look like the grand vision I had in my head. My childhood best friend, Mariah, and I sat in my kitchen looking for the best styling chairs, stations, and storage. One of my other best friends, Kathleen, and I scoured home stores for mirrors and accessories to add my personal touches. I planned for the capacity of eight stylists in the space and furnished it fully without the commitment or even a job posting for one stylist. Lesson learned!

I could have bought half of the furniture and equipment for the team I needed. I knew it would take time to be fully staffed. Instead of draining every penny of that check I worked so hard to save, I should have started with four stations, or even three, until I hired to fill them. I could have always added to the space upon hiring more, saving some of my initial investment capital for slow revenue, unplanned expenses, or incidentals. I should have planned to spend money as I was making it and been as conservative as possible with my investment capital. I prepared for three months of my overhead costs with that check, the money for a complete salon of equipment and furniture. It would have been best to keep more cash on hand for operating expenses and spend less on furnishings. A typical hire will be two weeks from commitment, allowing two weeks to purchase and receive a station and chair. Purchase your business essentials for the capacity you have plus ten percent, not the 100% capacity you're planning to reach.

My lessons learned did not stop when the salon opened, and I spent that big check. I made the same mistake of overspending a few times, thinking I was preparing myself. I stocked my retail shelves full of products like I would have booming foot traffic from day one. I spent thousands on products that sat on the shelves for months. At one point, I wanted to hire a nail technician when I relocated the salon to a new, non-subleased location. While interviewing, I bought tons of nail equipment to set up the space. My thought was to make the opportunity marketable for new hires by displaying that we were ready for them to join the team. One of my friends and now salon manager, Verdelle, told me to hold off spending money on all the nail products until we find the right fit for the position. She said they might have certain products they prefer, and we may take a long time to hire. She advised that we could be spending money now that we don't need to pay for months. She was right! We have yet to hire a nail technician. We used the nail table I bought as a receptionist desk. I later donated much of the nail supplies to a local cosmetology school after starting Lusso Gives, my non-profit 501c3 organization.

In all of these instances, I made these decisions based on putting out an image of flawless completion. That image would be attractive enough to drive success. Though the idea is essential, it is only some of what matters and is not the driving factor of any successful business. We must balance spending on enhancing the brand's image and prioritizing expenses. Clients did not flow in and out of the salon because I had a wall full of retail products. Once the clients did flow, retail sales didn't immediately peak either. It took time for potential customers to recognize and trust the brand before retuning and purchasing retail items. As my retail revenue increased, I increased my orders with suppliers.

Upon starting Lusso Extensions, my e-commerce store selling luxury human hair extensions, I made the mistake of overspending on inventory by having too many SKUs. This time my overspending was for a different reason than an image because this is all online. No one knows how much inventory you have in stock when customers are on your site. I overspent this time, thinking it would prepare me for any customer. I had five different hair textures at the time, frontals, closures, and all lengths of each. It was hundreds of SKUs. It was excessive for a new brand in a commodity market with no brand recognition. Now I know to use seasonal trends when ordering. As the warm weather approaches, it's the perfect time to stock up on shorter lengths for bobs and curly textures for wet looks. Stock up on longer lengths and sleek, straighter textures when it's cold. Offer pre-order sales when approaching the holidays or season changes so that people get a deal to order hair for their forthcoming hair plans and then place vendor orders using pre-order sales revenue. It took for me to overspend thousands on inventory and painfully watch it sit to understand how to use these strategies.

Notice I didn't say waste of money in any of these examples. I didn't waste the money. I still sold the inventory. I still used the furniture. I still sold the bundles. Therefore, I didn't waste my money. I mismanaged the money by spending it when it didn't need to be spent. Being strategic with your investment capital and managing expenses is a part of business ownership that separates a scaling business from a business that can only keep the doors open. Though I have learned many other lessons in the construction and startup venture of Lusso Suites, I did a better job managing controllable expenses that time. I ordered materials as they were needed. I did not over furnish. I did not purchase decor or specialty items before generating revenue. During that project, I remembered that it is ok to progress publicly. I like to think of Nike when I think of the progression of a brand. An image circulates on social media, often showing the evolution of their logo over the decades. That image portrays precisely this concept of public progression. Your business may not be fully baked when you get started. It never will be. That's what continuous improvement is about. Start with what you can comfortably afford.

You may not have it all on day one. Add things gradually. If your business is a brick-and-mortar, add finishing touches to enhance the look as you make money. I repainted my second location and added wallpaper and designer chandeliers when the business was making money to cover those expenses instead of digging into my savings. I am currently doing the same with Lusso Suites. Your faithful customers, employees, or contractors will notice those improvements too! They will make the assumption and connection to seeing those enhancements as business growth, giving them more confidence and commitment to your brand. It makes them have an intimate relationship with the brand because they can see the money they spend as a direct contribution to the growth of the business.

Don't Take It Personal

Aside from how I spent my money, I learned about managing business relationships. Everyone will not be as invested in your brand as you are. Some will give you their unwavering support and stick with you for the long term, but there will be others who will not. I knew this already, and I'm sure you do too, but what I had to learn the hard way is how to manage the emotions of these departures. When I receive compliments about my salon team's dedication and genuine camaraderie, I frequently remark that I had to kiss some frogs to get here. I've never done an interview where someone says, "this is just a stepping stone for me," or "I don't plan to work hard." Everyone is going to put their best foot forward first. Some people will even come in with the expectation to be a long-term contributor to your team but later find themselves going in another direction for no reason personal to your leadership or the opportunities you've provided. I've learned to remember there is a reason and a season for everyone in life, and it's no different when business is involved. When I see a client with their hair done and I know they have not been to Lusso Salon or a family member with a new sew-in, and I know they didn't place an order on *lussosalon.com* for extensions, I have learned to see that interaction differently in my mind rather than as failure.

Nothing is for face value. There can be many reasons you may not have been that person's choice this time, and it does not mean you won't ever be their choice in the future. Remind yourself it is not personal. Put on your CEO hat and evaluate the "why" in their decision. Do you meet their price point or availability? If you feel comfortable and have the relationship to ask, then do. Consider it business research, but what you mustn't do is blame yourself for the decisions of others or view their lack of support as a personal failure. The same goes for team retention. When you experience attrition on your team, instead of viewing it as a failure, use the opportunity to collect data points that will help you improve. Conduct an exit interview or send an exit survey to get ideas on what things can be improved within your business to retain the next hire better.

Taking things personally spun me to a dark, dangerous place. I started being extremely hard on myself and frankly obsessing over any potential penny lost instead of focusing on replicating the pennies earned. There were moments when I felt like a complete failure while neglecting to realize I had a business in front of me operating in the green with a team full of happy employees because I was too focused on the one bad review. For that one bad review, I'd have five that were amazing. Again with the self-sabotage. I'd make statements like "the business is going to shit" or "everything is failing." Those statements just were not factual, but were creating a dark cloud over my dream job. In those moments, I really relied on my village for support, but I've also learned ways to speak up for myself (again, therapy is fantastic). When I feel like a failure, I take out one of those cute notepads I told you about and fold a page in half. I write the shortcomings of the day (not failures) on one half and the wins on the other half. If the successes outweigh the drawbacks, then the day deserves a trophy. You must attend the trophy moment! Reward yourself in whatever way you need. For me, it's usually a long bubble bath at night, a stop at my favorite restaurant, splurging on a glass of wine at my favorite local wine bar, or a Dairy Queen dessert. Live in that joy! Admire your trophy on the shelf!

Let's be honest too. There will be some days when you screw up, and your list does not give you more wins than shortcomings. Unfortunately, you need to live in that too. This is when I put on my corporate senior manager hat. When I'd have an underperforming employee, it was part of the performance management process to write them a plan that gets them back on track. Who says you'll never need performance management just because you work for yourself? If you doubt your ability to handle this on your own, then leverage a leadership or business coach (shameless plug that is a service I offer), but before you spend money on that, here's a tip to taking a crack at it yourself. Now that you've written down the shortcomings, write a counteraction for each controllable defect that could have improved the situation. For an example of a fault: Inventory spend was more than what I expected for this order. Perhaps your counteraction can be:

- Compare the last four charges to identify slow-selling items and reduce SKUs in future orders.
- Take that counteraction and hold yourself accountable for doing it by a specific date.
- Put in whatever calendar you use.

Seriously, coach yourself if you don't do it just like you would for an employee.

For shortcomings that aren't controllable, for example, a software outage causing your website to be down or a power outage, write down an action plan for future occurrences so that if it ever happens again, you're not feeling panicked, frantic, or lost. Just because you are the boss and there is no one else to answer doesn't mean you don't need accountability. You may get assistance with these tactics from a business coach who will also encourage you to take responsibility for the objectives and plans you set. Still, you can also leverage a spouse, family member, or friend to be an accountability partner. Choose wisely; not everyone understands the mindset and challenges entrepreneurs face, so make sure to pick someone who can relate or is highly empathetic.

Realize that everyone will not understand this journey, which is only for some. People will ask you, "How's your little business going" or "Oh, you're still just doing...". Sometimes it will hurt because it may be the people closest to you who you expected to cheer the loudest. For those, understand that they mustn't have faith in your business like you do. They may have to see it to believe in it. As frustrating as it may be, they will come around when they start seeing some results. Until then, correct their comments and share with them your trophy moments. Make them see you! My favorite response is, "There's not much I do that is little. Thank you for asking. My business is doing great!" For those who are not close to you, just general naysayers, learn not to match their energy or let them bring you down. That's when you focus on the ten people who support you rather than those who don't. Put all your trophies on the shelf. Publicize them, share them, and show them off. As a full-time entrepreneur, there is no more promotion announcement on LinkedIn or Facebook when you reach a new milestone. You have to cheer loudly for yourself. You owe it to those who support you to include them in your business growth. It will just make them even more invested in you. When you cheer loudly for yourself more, you'll begin to hear more of those who are cheering with you than those who aren't.

Outsourcing

I learned that as we scale our businesses, we outsource to keep up. This outsourcing could be hiring a team or using contracted services. Just like anything else in business management, there is a balance needed. You cannot outsource too early. I made this mistake a few times, and it goes back to managing expenses. I didn't outsource much when I was dually employed for myself and Amazon because I couldn't afford much without digging into my personal pocket. At the time, I hired a family member of one of my stylists to be a virtual receptionist answering the few phone calls we were receiving because I could not answer them myself while at work. The business was new, and the number of clients coming in was low. We received about 10-20 phone calls per week, sometimes less, but I needed to outsource this. As I mentioned, I purely enjoyed my corporate career; even more so than enjoying it, I was good at it. Aside from my manager, who was highly supportive, and one of my close co-workers, none of my peers, and especially not my team at Amazon, knew I was starting a business. When I scheduled time to talk to my manager about the venture I was eager to pursue, I explained to her that if this would be a move that would jeopardize my job, it was not one I was ready to make. At the time of having this conversation, two months prior, I had recently been married, and I still had a few months before a significant promotion that I would be vying for. I will never forget what she told me. "The only way your decision to open a business would jeopardize your time here is if you make it by not performing the way you do now." She gave me a link to fill out for our legal team to keep track of employees who are also entrepreneurs and authenticate that there was no conflict of interest. Then I was on my way! I internalized her statement, and I didn't miss a beat. My job required frequent travel. I missed no meetings or on-site visits and got that promotion despite the pressures of running the business in my "off time." When I was away from the salon, I used cameras as my eyes and ears. I had tight reporting to keep track of sales and inventory and communicated with my team daily. At the time, I couldn't afford cleaning services, so I would come in after work to ensure the crew cleaned up behind themselves, and I'd come in on Sundays to do a deep cleaning. I was a one-woman band. Luckily I had a fantastic team who followed all the rules and processes. Many of them even would go above and beyond to do extra cleaning and closing tasks before they went home to help me out.

Choosing the time to outsource was about balance. The mistakes mentioned above of overspending had already been made, so now I was extremely frugal. I waited too late. I would get tired and not go in for inventory and deep cleaning on my day off. I ran employee payroll at midnight and arrived at the salon at 5 AM to finish things before opening. Verdelle came to me one day with the feedback that we needed a cleaning service. My team was exhausted from cleaning behind each other because that wasn't their job. I waited too long to leverage help, and this failure to realize sooner that it was time to outsource caused my team to suffer. They felt comfortable coming to me with this feedback, but it could have been very different. They could have just gotten frustrated with the issue and gone to another salon up the street. Those who know me also know I love reality TV, and one of my favorite shows is Bravo's Real Housewives of Atlanta. I thought of myself as I watched the episode where multimillionaire business owner, Kandi Burrs, told Sherree Whitfield about her struggle to launch her clothing business. One of the things she had to learn in business is that there is no successful, billion-dollar company where the CEO does everything with no team. We have to spend the money to hire support and outsource tasks that we can't do independently. This is why managing expenses is essential, as it helps keep the budget available for the resources you'd likely need in the future by not initially overspending on things you may not immediately need. We must endure the grind of doing it when getting started. You also don't want to outsource too soon and have more expenses than you can afford, but as you scale and grow, consider the low-hanging fruit that may help you get some of your time back for business planning. If you have a brick-and-mortar business, consider hiring someone to clean or work a register. For an e-commerce business, consider someone to help record inventory tracking or packing orders. Outsourcing can also be software, like paying for a virtual reception service, online booking, or online calendar service to assist in managing client leads. If you're stretched thin working easily replicated tasks, there's no way you can give your all to scaling your business.

CHAPTER 4

CHALLENGES

Life is meaningless if we aren't learning, right? I keep learning a lot in this self-employed journey, which certainly doesn't come without challenges. Some of those challenges have contributed to self-doubt, but many are my motivation to keep improving the business to make it easier for me.

Balance

How do we balance being a wife, mom, daughter, friend, and business owner while caring for ourselves? I've shared this little tactic of mine a few times during speaking engagements, and people have looked at me like I'm insane, but for me, it works. I go back to those darn notebooks again! I have one in my desk drawer for my formula. As I am a business-minded person and extremely analytical (maybe sometimes too analytical), I create my balance using a formula I write down. We can all only give 100%, so that's what is behind the equal sign in the equation. I provide each significant aspect of my life with a variable. Let's call the business

L, M for marriage, Z for my child, H for household tasks, and C for myself. I lump friends and family in with myself because my friends encompass my social life, which is super important to me. I'm an extrovert. When I am not social, my thermometer is low, and I am not at my best. The same goes for when I do not have enough time for my family or self-care and maintenance. Now that everything has a variable, I have to solve for each to equal 100%. If my husband has a lot on his plate with work or his personal life that requires me to tap in, maybe variable M needs 50%, leaving another 50% for all the other variables. During times when the business has been hemorrhaging or during the company's expansion to Lusso Suites, the L variable may be up to 60% at that time, leaving only 40% for everything else. My daughter has many activities. At one point, she had soccer, dance, and band while adjusting to some challenging courses in her middle school curriculum, requiring that we stay close to her study habits and homework routines. During that time, variable Z needed a higher percentage than all others. No matter what, the equation cannot exceed 100%.

So, how does this help? After giving each variable its percentage to your week, the next step is to translate that into hours. 168 hours make up a week, of which I commit to sleeping for 56 of them; for me, that is non-negotiable. My commute, time to get dressed, and eating deduct another 14 hours from my week, leaving me 98 hours for my crazy equation here.

I always estimate down to account for the things I can't easily fit into these variables; therefore, I plan my week at 95 hours. For example, if my business gets 50% of my productive time for the week, I am planning to give it 47.5 hours.

It all sounds crazy and so structured, but this works not because I stick to it and track it like crazy but because it helps me have a plan. This is just how I build my calendar for the week, making me conscious of being out of balance. This method helps me to be aware if I am on borrowed time. One area where I always struggle is balancing 'the C variable" during the summertime. I want to go on trips, hang out at the pool, go to a bar with friends after work, and sleep late. There is no homework to focus on with my daughter, so her variable is easy during the summertime, leaving me more time for myself. The struggle comes when I need to be more motivated to work and sometimes fill every weekend with social activities instead of quality time with my hubby. I change my equation during the summer months to be realistic about what's in front of me, and when I deviate. Having the equation helps me be hyper-aware that I need to spend a little more time elsewhere.

Another good trick I sometimes use is to lower my weekly productive hours. Instead of 98, plan for 90 during some months giving yourself more time for sleep or idle time. You can always beef it up when it's time to grind again. During the back-to-school period,

I always plan for my daughter and marriage variables to eat a little more of my productive time in the week because our schedules and routines are dynamic, activities start up again, and there is homework to do. We are usually also more active in the house, meaning that housework time may increase too.

For me, the point of this method is not to become obsessed with the accuracy of the numbers nor to take a lot of time or extreme measures to ensure you're sticking to it but to shift your awareness to your capacity. I started doing this while balancing the business startup with my Amazon career. I wouldn't allow Amazon to be less than 50% of my week because I did not want to underperform at work. This method helped me craft my schedule and manage my calendar with colors. Every variable has a color, and it gives me a visual of the time I have available. I use Google Calendar, and I swear by it. Even my housework time is on that calendar in its respective color for the number of hours I've planned for the week. Do I stick to it every week? Nope! But with this, I know I'll need to ask for help to get it done or outsource a service to pick up the slack. At one point, I was redoing the equation week to week and updating my calendar. Now things are more routine, and I don't do this more than quarterly or monthly.

What happens when 100% isn't enough? What happens when you can't fit it into your allotted productive hours? Simple. You have to say no and ask for help or outsource service as long as it's within your budget. While working on the Lusso Suites project, my daughter was starting her soccer season but still participating in band and dance. I was volunteer coaching for a cheerleading team over the summer; it falls in the variable "C" for myself. As much as I loved it, I had to drop it. My equation couldn't exceed 100% by keeping that activity. These are the sacrifices we have to make, especially as entrepreneurs.

When life gets hectic or stressful, we still have to meet the demands of the business. This is what I had to adjust to the outside of a corporate environment. When working for a corporation, the show doesn't stop if you're not performing well; you simply get replaced. You can't replace yourself when running a small business (at least not one at this scale). When life sucks, you've still got to keep the lights on at your company. You still have to send out the orders and hunt for engagement on social media. The hustle and bustle don't stop. I run my team's payroll on Tuesdays. Whether I am out of town, sick, or tired, if I don't run the payroll on Tuesday, my team will not get paid on time, which isn't an option. You can't neglect your relationship or your children if you have one. You also must pay attention to yourself. That's the importance of the equation. It's simply an exercise of a conscious attempt to have balance and order to a hectic life load.

Money

Some people think that being a business owner means having an abundant supply of cash. They assume you must be rich based on your business, the fact that you have employees, the story you paint for social media to promote your business, and maybe the lifestyle they think you live. Let's be real… that is not true. There are substantial personal financial challenges that come with being an entrepreneur. I had never missed a bill in my life until I was self-employed. There were times when the business underperformed in important sales goals, and as the business owner, it fell on me to pick up the slack. I could leverage extra clients or run an e-commerce sale for Lusso Extensions for some last-minute revenue, but if business goals weren't met, that is not money I'd put in my pocket. Even after paying myself anything extra, I'd use it to reinvest in the business. All you know about consistent income is in the rearview mirror, which also changes how you manage money in your personal life. I had to learn how to strike a balance. Remember earlier in this book when I mentioned using my husband's laptop? Now I'm going to tell you why. This is one of the methods I used to create a balance between reinvesting in the business and paying myself; I'm going to call it the 'thermometer method.'

I wrote down business needs that could solve a problem or grow the business. One of which was a new front desk computer. At the business's inception, I bought a MacBook to create my business plan and get started. I also purchased an iPad, Square Stand, and POS processing equipment for our front desk. As the business grew, we hired an in-house receptionist, as more than the iPad was needed to manage inventory and internal tasks. I started carrying my MacBook to work with me daily for the salon team to use. I couldn't afford to purchase an iMac for the front desk. To avoid a situation whereby the team required a computer, but there wasn't one available because I wasn't around, My husband, who is also my biggest supporter, told me to leave my MacBook at the salon to use his at home when I needed to.

What happened is that I completely took his MacBook. It started to live on my desk or in my bag. At one point, I couldn't even recall the last time he used it. This was when I came up with the thermometer method. I again used one of those cute little notebooks and drew my rendition of a thermometer with a monetary target to meet before purchasing the iMac. This goal was profit-based, meaning an amount of money sitting in the bank after all overhead expenses were paid and after I paid myself. This was my way of striking balance. I could no longer shovel every dollar back into the business. There was no corporate income to fall back on. After all, I had my expenses and... you know, life. The thermometer kept me from shorting myself while reinvesting into the business. This is a perfect example of when I used it because the iMac is unnecessary. We had a computer to use, and I had one at home. If worse came to worst, I'd keep carrying my MacBook to and from work daily. Would it be inconvenient? Sure, but it would work. Once getting to the profit goal I needed, then I'd get the shiny new thing. I started using thermometers for so many wants for the business. I wanted to repaint the salon's interior, get chandeliers and put up wallpaper. I made a thermometer for it. Once I hit the goal, I was in action. I wanted new shampoo chairs for the wet bar; I made a thermometer. I could visualize a strategy to strive to get the things I want without draining my accounts or straining myself.

This method only worked for enhancements to the business and wants. This was it for things that would be nice to have. When it comes to things that create operational barriers that impact the bottom line, it is wise not to wait for goals but to execute them. For example, the salon laundry dryer stopped working right after Christmas (the worst time ever for my budget). In this industry, it's also a time when we are preparing for a slow period with client flow. Even though it was not great timing, we can only operate smoothly with a laundry washer and dryer because we must continuously launder towels and capes throughout the day. I decided to replace it, which would have cost nearly the same amount as waiting to repair it, ordering a second batch of towels to rotate, and using a wash and fold laundromat service daily, causing an uphill task for my salon manager. Not to mention, the additional expense of the laundromat.

When it comes to things that will stop the clock or cause discomfort for the team, they have to be addressed right away, and to me, that may mean digging into my pocket or in the profit savings, therefore, causing a decrease to the fill of one of my thermometers. At that point, the decision becomes which pocket we will use.

My thermometers also helped me to know when it was an excellent time to expand. Once I reached a specific financial profit goal, I was comfortable pursuing Lusso Suites, the first multifunctional micro storefront rental location of the Lusso Brand. Seeing a visual representation of reaching my goals was incredibly motivating to me.

Patience

I am the world's most impatient person. I know that is terrible, but it is true. I want to fulfill all those dreams I wrote down at the beginning of this book, like... yesterday. I mean, why isn't Own Network knocking on my door yet to add me to the cast of their new reality show? I think, as an entrepreneur, we are full of ideas about our businesses. We can vibrantly see this empire of a business, but we have the barrier of time, money, and resources to accomplish it all. My dreams for my business are vivid and sometimes keep me awake at night. I can see the next location opening or the speaking engagement I hope to keynote. I cannot pretend to be an expert on conquering this constant hamster wheel of impatience because it is my biggest challenge. My husband has helped me shake my anxiety when I think the business isn't moving forward enough for me. We start to list all the things we have accomplished. Be detailed! List them out and get granular. It is going to make you think of how far you have come. The amount of time isn't even going to feel important. That reflection makes me pause and revel in the success I've seen thus far. It helps me to stop feeling I haven't done enough yet. Suddenly all of the other things I want to get done seem more attainable, and I'm content with taking the time needed to get them done.

Being overly impatient has made me rush decisions about the business, which has caused me difficulties. There have been times when I've pulled the trigger on projects before the thermometer is filled because I am trying to balance striking while the iron is hot with making thoughtful business decisions. Sometimes, even with a filled thermometer, I made decisions without fully baked plans. The most impactful moment I can think of where my impatience has impacted me was with the launch of the Lusso Extensions e-commerce store. I went into this venture virtually with no plan. I got a logo, created a website, and overspent on inventory. I needed to develop adequate sales goals and plan how to package orders. I started spending money on ads left and right without doing much research on how to optimize them. After months of wasting money on ads and thousands of dollars in inventory, I was ready to throw the towel on the entire business. Patience is the virtue I was missing in this. I should have waited until I had a complete plan and done the research necessary to know how to make the business successful. Now that time has passed, and I have learned many lessons, I can navigate through the industry successfully, but it took lots of frustration and correction to get there due to rushed decision-making and poor planning. Once I saw the website coming together and started receiving inventory and packaging orders in the mail, I couldn't delay the success I knew would be inevitable. Having the self-control to wait for optimal timing is essential. This doesn't mean waiting for perfection because you will genuinely wait forever if that is the case. Remember, brands evolve, grow and change, just like the Nike example. However, this doesn't mean we should jump off the ledge before we have tested the cord.

CHAPTER 5

LITTLE BLACK BOOK

It's safe to say I'm obsessed with notebooks... LOL. One of the handy dandy notebooks I call the Little Black Book has traveled with me for over a decade. It's not the Little Black Book you may be thinking of. This is a bookkeeping note from all the salons I've worked in throughout my life. I started it at my first job in middle school, and I have it to this day. Anytime I am asked by an aspiring business owner for advice during the early stages of business planning, I tell them to keep a Little Black Book. In this book, I wrote down everything I liked and didn't like about every salon where I worked. I wrote simple observations about what things went well and what didn't. My intentions were not to forget what things I'd like to implement in my salon. This could apply to any business. Let's say you want to own a restaurant; even if you haven't worked in one, I'm sure you have been a customer. Track what impresses you, and jot down your ideas; that way, when you're business planning, you aren't lost to things you want to incorporate. At one salon where I worked, there were multiple shampoo assistants. They had a rotation list at the front desk, which dictated who was next to shampoo at any given time. This kept the flow of work balanced and fair. At a different salon, the shampoo assistants were assigned a stylist for the day based on everyone's schedule.

I wouldn't say I liked this because if the stylist you happened to be assigned to had a slow day, so did you, and the neighboring assistant might have been overworked and needed help. I took notes of these things to make them best practices at Lusso Salon. One of the most impactful to me is our wait times. Lusso Salon is known for respecting clients' time by ensuring wait times are less than 15 minutes. On the rare occasion, we should exceed 15 minutes, and we make it a standard to call the client before their appointment begins to make them aware of the delay and ask that they come later. I picked up this simple routine from observing how agitated clients become with excessive wait times at other salons. It has become part of The Lusso Brand reputation by notating this, creating a plan, and training my team on this expectation.

Annually, usually before the first of the year, I revisit the Little Black Book, and I've added Lusso Salon. I have written down the things I dislike about the business operation. It's a critical part of self-reflection. This year, one of the things I wrote down that I love about my business is the team dynamic. We have a team of people who care about each other and are invested in the business's success. My last two occurrences of attrition were from stylists who chose to open their businesses rather than because they were underperforming or dissatisfied with the environment. That is a huge win! I have identified that I would like to change our inventory management this year. We arbitrarily order products as we see them running low, and my team seems to think there is no budget for these orders. I will keep these things at the forefront of my goals for the new year. I should focus on continuing to do the things that have built my team's rapport. To eliminate overspending and product waste, I should also take time to problem-solve our inventory management system or lack thereof. Identifying wins and gaps in your business often is a way to drive continuous improvement.

CHAPTER 6

THE ROLODEX

There are a host of influential people with whom every small business owner needs to have a strong relationship. I call it your Rolodex. Within your Rolodex, you need the following:

- CPA
- A Law Firm
- Collections Agency (depending on your business)
- Virtual Assistant
- Fiduciary or Insurance Agent

Some people to also consider could be:

- Business Coach or Leadership Coach
- Social Media Manager
- Bookkeeper

You're probably thinking, "How can I possibly

pay all these people and not outsource too early, as we mentioned earlier in this book?". This may seem like a long list, but let me explain. Though, as the rockstar CEO you are, you will be excellent at wearing multiple hats, some things will cost you a ton of extra money if you get them wrong. These people, as mentioned above, do not have to be on your payroll, but they are people you should have access to and can call when you need them. When you're ready to open your business, schedule a consultation with a few CPAs. During these consultations, feel them out for their expertise and ask them what they need for optimal working relationships based on your business. Many CPAs do these consultations complimentary to earn your business, and they will tell you what types of reporting you need to keep for your business type and your business formation to file annual taxes with them. Not only will you get some advice to start things organized, but when you're ready to file your taxes, you will already know how much it'll cost and to whom to go. Have that person in your Rolodex so you can call on them when you need to get this done.

I recommend doing the same with a law firm. As part of your startup research, you must have a law firm in your Rolodex should a need for them arise. Notice I said a firm and not just a lawyer. One lawyer will have an area of law that they practice. It would be best if you worked with a company that can manage legal concerns related to several issues. Look for a firm that works with small businesses on trademark issues, liability, or negligence defense, and schedule a consultation to introduce yourself and your business this way. You have someone to turn to in case of legal matters while operating your business. Nothing is worse than finding yourself in legal trouble and starting from scratch, confused about who to call for help.

If you have a business type that collects money from clients, you will want to have a collections agency in your Rolodex. You may never need to use them, but you will want to know one to pivot quickly in case you need to. My business collects booth rent. If I ever have a stylist with outstanding booth rent and I need help closing a delinquent account, I have a collections agency in my Rolodex. I did consultations with three different agencies, and I learned a lot during each consultation. They told me what thresholds I needed to meet before I could collect with their services, how much they keep in fees from collections, and how long it typically takes to close a case. To this day, I have never had to use the agency, but I started a relationship with them. I have a contact I can email if I need to, and I am informed of the process. If I ever find myself in a situation where someone owes me outstanding booth rent, I will not feel frantic about what to do next because I am well aware of the process. It also helped me to know and proactively add the information I was missing in my contract to protect myself and facilitate successful collections.

We are in the virtual age where needing to

leverage help for services no longer requires paying someone to sit with you in person in an office. It's essential to have a virtual assistant in your Rolodex who you can leverage for help when you are burdened with tasks you cannot complete on your own. Reach out to a few and have discovery consultations to learn what services they offer, how to retain them, and their costs. You may find yourself shocked where you can afford to reach out for some help as a le cart expense in a busy month.

Having a fiduciary or insurance agent is super important. I started my relationship with my fiduciary while I was working for Amazon. He set me up with investments that grew. I could utilize the money I had stowed away to grow my business. I encourage you to speak with a few to find someone who fits your needs. Typically, a fiduciary sells insurance plans as well. As your business grows and you have employees, they can ensure you're up-to-date on what types of insurance you need to comply with labor laws. They can also shop for the best plans to fit your budget and needs. Like the other services we discussed, starting a relationship with a fiduciary is typically free of cost. I have never paid out of pocket for his help and guidance. They make money based on the products you elect to use from them, therefore not resulting in costly monthly payments or extra bills.

Consultations with a business or leadership coach, social media manager, and bookkeeper are ones you should also consider. My business coaching consultations are complimentary, so I can get to know the business and see if we're a good fit. During the consultation, you can learn when to leverage help from the coach and what types of services they offer so that if you ever find yourself in a rut, you already know where to turn. These consultations can be informative, where you collect some gems and have some knowledge of what resources you have. Some virtual assistants offer social media management, but if the ones you've decided to connect with do not, find someone who does and find out what tools they'd need from you to assist. The same goes for bookkeeping. Some virtual assistants do bookkeeping, but some don't. A discovery call with a bookkeeper will tell you how to set up your business's financial reporting to allow someone to hop in and help.

Starting your business with a Rolodex will make you confident that you're not operating alone. Even if you cannot afford their services immediately, you know how much they cost, have started a relationship, and are not scrambling to find someone when you need them. You're going to thank yourself for getting started in a way that allows you to scale. If you know exactly what a CPA or bookkeeper needs, for example, but aren't ready to use one yet, you can operate your business in a way that when you can afford those services, it will be plug-and-play to have that help quickly and easily. Keep yourself from a scramble at a time of need. Also, you'll learn a lot during these consultations, making yourself a more educated CEO.

CHAPTER 7

THE BEST PART

Despite all the challenges, I am doing what I was called to do. I do not regret leaping off the corporate ladder. I've discovered a lot about myself, and I can fulfill my passion while also making money to live a fantastic lifestyle. Being a CEO has many benefits, one of which is the freedom to make important choices without seeking approval from an employer. I can change my schedule or change my pay as I need. I can take time off or change my work focus. During the school months, my schedule in the salon to service clients is from 7 AM to 2 PM during the weekdays. This schedule allows me to get home from work at the same time as my daughter's school bus, assist her with her homework, and cook dinner. This also allows me to take her to any of her after-school activities. Being a present mother and wife is essential to me. Being an entrepreneur has allowed me to invest more of my time where I see fit. This isn't to say that those who work in corporate environments cannot be present mothers. This also doesn't mean that there aren't times when, as an entrepreneur, I don't struggle to find the time to be present at home, but it does make this easier for me because I can do things on my own time, my way. What I didn't understand was the reason why I was still not 100% happy. I have the privilege of living my dreams, so what is the problem?! What is next?

I realized I was not feeling fulfilled because I had not yet truly tapped into my inner CEO. I was simply managing a business without the overwhelming feeling of balancing a corporate job. Though this was a weight lifted, I was not giving my full potential to growing my business as I envisioned because I was trapped in the cycle of grinding to supplement the income I lost from a corporate salary. I was substituting much of my once corporate working hours with servicing clients, not scaling my business or developing the brand. I didn't quit my job to be a hairstylist. I quit my job to be a boss with a recognizable, franchised business. Choosing a business where my passion lies has been essential to my motivation through these low moments. When I feel like I made a mistake in this choice or I am moving too slowly in achieving my goals, passion pulls me through. If I weren't passionate about cosmetology and my brand, I would have given up the first time I over drafted my checking account after spending my last on payroll during a low revenue month. The fulfillment I receive in this comes from my passion and love for what I am doing, not from chasing a dollar. It's the most necessary part of my success.

This year I am focusing on growing my brand. I've invested my heart and soul into my company and helped my team members build successful careers. Now it is your time! Pursuing your dreams does not have to be on the back burner. Start that business plan. Start that website. Start that product line or clothing brand! You will thank yourself later. I started Lusso Experience Salon and Spa LLC in 2014, five years before opening a physical location. I went to my dad and told him about my dreams while I was in college. He sat down with me and created my LLC because he believed in me. He pushed me hard and always has. Surround yourself with a circle of people who can believe in your dreams with you. Having such people in my corner made a difference for me. At times when I have been ready to give up or felt like I would never be able to achieve my goals, my husband, family, and friends were able to push me. They say it's lonely at the top. That may be partially true, but it doesn't have to be. Your circle may have to change. There are like-minded CEO bosses out there just like you! You have to put yourself in places to network with and embrace new people who will encourage you.

It is more than rewarding to see your dreams come to fruition, and it's simply fulfilling, no matter how long it takes. I have had the privilege of loving what I do daily, and so should you. I was not able to call it all quits at once. It took time for me to make realistic plans to live a life pursuing my passion, but if I'd never made the plan, I would not be this close. I am not there yet! I still have achievements awaiting. My book is still being written. Start writing yours and leap off the ladder!

Made in the USA
Middletown, DE
31 March 2023